Barrymore

by
William Luce

Barrymore

A New Play by
WILLIAM LUCE

GARDEN CITY, NEW YORK

Design by Maria Chiarino
Manufactured in the U.S.A.
ISBN: 1-56865-439-1

BARRYMORE was originally produced at the Stratford Festival in Ontario, Canada, as a first collaboration between the Festival and Garth H. Drabinsky's LIVENT INC. It opened on September 20, 1996, starring Christopher Plummer, featuring Michael Mastro, and directed by Gene Saks. Scenic and costume design were by Santo Loquasto and the production stage manager was Susan Konynenburg.

The production subsequently toured several cities in the United States, then opened on Broadway at the Music Box Theatre on March 25, 1997. Mr. Plummer won a Tony® Award as Best Actor for his portrayal of John Barrymore.

Cast

(in order of appearance)

John Barrymore . . . . . . CHRISTOPHER PLUMMER

Prompter . . . . MICHAEL MASTRO

The play takes place one month before John Barrymore's death.

Act I The spring of 1942

Act II Later the same evening

AUTHOR'S ACKNOWLEDGEMENTS
The author acknowledges the use of excerpts from the following authors: William Shakespeare, Lord Byron, Oliver Goldsmith, Frances Thompson, Robert Browning, Eugene Field and Wilson MacDonald.

GRATEFUL ACKNOWLEDGEMENT
IS MADE TO **WILL FOWLER** FOR
HIS GENEROUS CO-OPERATION
IN SUPPLYING BASIC MATERIAL
FOR THIS PLAY FROM HIS
BOOKS, ARTICLES AND PERSONAL
REMEMBRANCES OF
JOHN BARRYMORE.

Author's Notes

John Barrymore was already the most popular actor in America when he decided to try his hand at Shakespeare. The year was 1920. He was thirty-eight, the young brother of Ethel and Lionel Barrymore—all three, heirs to an acting dynasty, unwilling recruits into the family business. Behind John Barrymore lay many theatrical hits and flops—some roles trifling, others serious and undisputedly praiseworthy—plus a good number of silent films. In his public's estimation, he was a matinee idol of romantic mien, handsome proportion and profile; possessed of a roving eye and a colorful reputation for high-jinx. Critics and audiences were thus taken by surprise when their quintessential "leading man" lurched onto New York's Plymouth Theatre stage as the warped and malevolent Richard III. Observed Barrymore's vocal coach, Margaret Carrington, "Jack's was a demonstration of demoniac talent at its highest pitch."

Yet, a greater test of his actor's mettle lay ahead. Within three years, he assayed the character of Hamlet in a performance which came to be considered the first great enactment of the role in this century. Sensitive, simple, modern in interpretation, he ran long enough to break Edwin Booth's New York record. Then he took London by storm. Recalled Laurence Olivier, "Everything about him was exciting. He was athletic, he had charisma and, to my young mind, he played the part to perfection. He was astounding." With the closing of *Hamlet*, the high pitch of Jack's "demoniac talent" had spent itself.

Although some creditable film performances followed, alcoholism and self-mockery claimed the rest of his career; his real-life Falstaffian behavior all but obliterated the memory of his shining hour as a magnificent actor. Moreover, the business of theater no longer tolerated the indulgences upon which Jack fed in order to make his art possible. Brooks Atkinson said, "John Barrymore was Icarus who flew so close to the sun that the wax on his wings melted and he plunged

AUTHOR'S NOTES

back to earth—from the peak of classical acting to the banalities of show business."

That Jack's decline was pathetic is true. That it was tragic is debatable. He had seized the moment, experienced an artistic "high" known to few. Perhaps the one tragic thing would have been his *not* daring the flight "close to the sun."

—William Luce

For Christopher Plummer

Act One

ACT I

As house goes to black, a single shaft of shimmering light appears, as if floating midair. Out of some memory, the voice of John Barrymore as Antony roars with laughter and speaks.

BARRYMORE *(taped)*:
    Come, my friends,
    There's sap in't yet. The next time I do fight
    I'll make death love me; Come,
    Let's have one other gaudy night: call to me
    All my sad captains, fill our bowls; once more
    Let's mock the midnight bell.

(We are in a New York theater, 1942. A bare light bulb burns on a metal standard. A hulking shape is seen, covered by a canvas. It is actually a throne, which will be used in the second act. Now it is indistinguishable. The stage is otherwise bare, except for three chairs, a large wicker trunk on which sit a bowl of red apples and a book of Shakespeare; a full-length mirror, victrola and records; a small barrel containing swords, canes and a fly swatter. Barrymore, in a suit and hat, enters, pulling a garment rack hung with Richard III costumes. He is modestly inebriated)

BARRYMORE *(singing)*:
    A B C D E F G H I got a gal in Kalamazoo,
    Don't wanna boast, but I know she's the toast
    Of Kalamazoo, zoo, zoo, zoo, zoo, zoo—

(Reciting to audience)

Yolanda in Kalamazoo
Once strolled after dark by the zoo.
She was seized by the nape
And humped by an ape,
As she sighed, "What a heavenly screw."

Just a minute. I forgot the baby.
(*Singing, he exits*)
I'm gonna send a wire, hoppin' on a flyer, leavin'
today.
Am I dreamin'; I can hear her screamin'—
(*À la Ted Lewis*)
Is everybody happy?

(*He re-enters with a small black doctor's bag*)

(*Singing*)
A B C D E F G H I got a gal in Kalamazoo—
(*To audience*)
My medicinal bag. It goes where I go. Its only objec-
tionable feature is that people are convinced I carry
around my own ashes. It actually contains vital, life-
sustaining potions from my pharmacist at the Jungle
Club on Seventh Avenue.

(*From the bag he removes two whiskey bottles*)

(*Singing*)
Years have gone by; my, my, how she grew;
I liked her looks, when I carried her books in Kal-
amazoo, zoo, zoo, zoo—
(*Reciting to audience*)
Said Yolanda, "Oh, my, you're so hairy!

4

But I hope—yes, I do—that I marry
A man with a schlong
Half as thick and as long
As the kind that you zoo-keepers carry."

I must be a frigging masochist and, God knows, an egotist—for here I am, three months after the attack on Pearl Harbor, the whole world at war, and I'm trying to revive my puny career. As well try to rejuvenate my sex life and turn this limp noodle into a bushwhacker.

I can't believe I forked out good money to rent this God-forsaken dump for one night, just to run a few goddamned lines. But I have, so do not be put off by the disarray that you see. All this will hopefully be transformed into the throne room of that lump of foul deformity, ruthless Richard the Turd.

God, he was shit, wasn't he? But I have an affinity with shits.

You know, Richard was my first real success as a classical actor. It was long ago, but it was the first time they took me seriously. So I've got to try to get the old bastard up on his feet again. I need to be taken seriously once more before the man in the bright nightgown comes for me.

That is, if my trusty prompter ever arrives. For the success of this hazardous enterprise rests not only on your approval, but on the shaky ability of an aging actor to remember his lines. And if, perchance, there

BARRYMORE

are among you one or two charitable angels, the smallest gesture will not be unwelcome. Thank you—

(*He extends his upturned hat to the audience*)

Thank you, thank you, thank you—
(*To audience member*)
Hya, Mister Jackson—
(*Singing*)
Ev'rything's O K A L A M A Z O
Oh, what a gal, a real piperoo.
I'll make my bid for that freckle-face kid I'm hurrying to.
I'm goin' to Michigan to see the sweetest gal in—
(*To audience*)
Have you ever seen delirium tremens? A colleague of mine, a bibulous fellow thespian, had the best DTs I've ever seen. You might say, Henry's bladder abhorred a vacuum. Henry Malcolm Rogers, known in theater circles as the world's best worst actor. He kicked the bucket last week at sixty-two, but not from liquor. He died of what in New York is called a natural death—he was hit by a cab.

Hank drank a quart of whiskey a day for forty years. They tried to cremate him, but he blew up and wrecked the place. Dear Henry, the only man I ever knew with varicose veins in his eyeballs.

There's really nothing funny about booze. (*Laughing a boozy laugh*) Hell, I must be a living advertisement for all the friggin' liquor companies in the world.

Look at these—(*Extending trembling hands*) Restless little buggers, aren't they? I'm so far gone, I haven't left yet. But things are beginning to click for me— my knees, my elbows, my neck. When I get out of bed, I sound like Carmen Miranda's castanets.

But I don't feel old yet. They say a man isn't old till regrets take the place of dreams. That's it, isn't it? Dreams. And then our little life is rounded with a sleep, blood clots, gout, arthritis, dropsy, ulcers and—oh, yes—hemorrhoids. They're a pain in the neck. (*Holding up banana*) The sovereign panacea for whiskey breath.

A tippler from Riverside Drive
Had breath you could barely survive.
He ate a banana,
Read George Santayana,
Then farted Chanel No. 5.

Allow me to disabuse you of the prevalent notion that Jack Barrymore is a tragic figure. I do not suffer easily those maudlin sob-sisters who lament my fall from grace. Hell, they haven't even got the decency to wait till I die. Get this straight: I've had one hell-uva life—for a man who's been dead fifteen years.

(*He finds a flyswatter in the barrel*)

You know, one summer holiday on Staten Island, my brother Lionel and I staged furious duels with these. I was six—I was the baby. Lionel was ten. My sister Ethel, who was nine going on forty, saw us showing off and got the idea of putting on a play in the barn behind the boarding house. All thirty-seven guests came. Each paid a penny. I earned six cents. Lionel, ten. Ethel kept the remaining twenty-one cents for herself. Star billing and production costs. Lionel was irate, threatened to quit. But I was completely happy, because I hadn't learned to count yet.

(*He peers into the barrel*)

Jesus Christ! *I* must be having the DTs. What the hell is that? (*Pause*) Oh, it's only a glove. I thought it was a dead rat—which reminds me of my father. That bastard. He used to drag me along on his nightly binges. I wasn't even ten yet. He'd stumble home at dawn without me—forgot all about me. Just left me in some dingy whorehouse. The girls were always telling me how cute I was, how much I looked like my father.

I was damned if I was going to be like him. That lunatic. He was a madman, a brute—and he got worse. Once he almost killed Ethel—had her by the throat, then ran off screaming into the night. I chased him for twenty blocks. I didn't give a shit how big he was. I was going to kill that raving son-uvabitch.

Is that my inheritance? Scares the hell out of me.

(*Stage lights are turned on*)

What's going on?

(*The prompter, Frank, speaks from offstage*)

PROMPTER: That you, sir?

BARRYMORE: It is I, be not afeard. Who calls?

PROMPTER: Frank. Let me know when you want to start running your lines. I'm all set up and ready to go.

BARRYMORE (*to audience*): Well! Mr. Efficiency has finally turned up. (*To prompter*) Hello, Frank.

PROMPTER: Hello, sir.

BARRYMORE: How've you been?

PROMPTER: Fine, sir.

BARRYMORE: Keeping busy?

PROMPTER: Yes.

BARRYMORE (*to audience*): That's our Frank. (*To prompter*) Still living in Yonkers?

PROMPTER: Yes.

BARRYMORE: With your mother?

PROMPTER: Yes.

BARRYMORE: How is she?

PROMPTER: So-so.

BARRYMORE: What?

PROMPTER: So-so.

BARRYMORE: That's life. (*To audience*) Dear old Frank. I have but to discreetly cradle my auditory orifice, lean artfully in his direction, murmur, "Line?" and the forgotten words waft their way toward my eagerly awaiting ear, unbeknownst to the enchanted audience.

PROMPTER: Anytime, Mr. Barrymore.

BARRYMORE (*having a swig*): I have very poor and unhappy brains for drinking: I could well wish courtesy would invent some other custom of entertainment.

PROMPTER: Wait a minute, sir.

BARRYMORE: Hmm?

PROMPTER: That's not from *Richard.*

BARRYMORE: Oh? How perceptive of you, Frank. What *is* it from?

PROMPTER: *Othello.*

BARRYMORE: Right as usual. (*To audience*) Pedantic prick. Save me from him. (*As Richard*) A horse! A horse! My kingdom for a horse!

PROMPTER: Mr. Barrymore, aren't we taking it from the beginning?

BARRYMORE (*to prompter*): Presumably.

PROMPTER: That's the *end* of the play.

BARRYMORE (*to audience*): Tedious boy. (*To prompter*) All right, Frank.

PROMPTER: Act one, scene one.

BARRYMORE: Give me a second here. Right. Start me off.

PROMPTER: Now—

BARRYMORE: Now's as good a time as any.

PROMPTER: No. "Now" is the first word.

BARRYMORE: Oh.

PROMPTER: Now is the—

BARRYMORE: Now is the *what?* Now is the *what?*

PROMPTER: Now is the winter of—

BARRYMORE: Now is the *winter* of what?

PROMPTER: Our discontent.

BARRYMORE: Now is the winter of our discontent—
(*Annoyed*) That's what I said! Don't you listen, boy?

PROMPTER: I listen!

BARRYMORE: Frank, don't prompt me unless I ask. If I
ever need one, I will just say, "Line." (*Pause*) Line.

PROMPTER: By this sun of York—

BARRYMORE: Line.

PROMPTER: And all the clouds that lour'd—

BARRYMORE (*taking over*): —that lour'd upon our
house
In the deep bosom of the ocean buried.

God, that was a killer. Let's take a break.

PROMPTER: You've only done four lines.

BARRYMORE: Oh, shut up, Frank.

PROMPTER: Come on, Mr. Barrymore, let's get serious.

BARRYMORE: All right, Simon Legree. What's next?

PROMPTER: Now are our brows—

BARRYMORE: Now are our brows—(*To audience*) I can
recite two entire plays by Shakespeare. I know

you've heard that when I make pictures, I use black-boards once in awhile, placed in strategic positions.

PROMPTER: Bound with victorious wreathes—

BARRYMORE: Well, it's true! What the hell's wrong with that?

PROMPTER: Bound with victorious wreathes—

BARRYMORE (*to prompter*):   Shut up, Frank. (*To audience*) Doesn't mean I'm losing my marbles, does it?

PROMPTER (*impatiently*):   Bound with victorious wreaths!

BARRYMORE (*to prompter*):   That's right, keep after me!

PROMPTER: Come on!

BARRYMORE (*to audience*):   See? Never gives up. To-night all is well. Franklin is at the helm.

(*He reaches for a bottle*)

PROMPTER: What're you doing? You know what the manager says.

BARRYMORE (*to prompter*):   I do not give a rat's ass what the manager says.

PROMPTER: No drinking on the premises.

BARRYMORE (*as Gertrude, to bottle*): No, no, the
drink, the drink,—O my dear Hamlet,—
The drink, the drink!—I am poison'd.

(*To himself*)

Maybe I should do Hamlet. No, no. Too late, too old.
Alas, Richard is an undertaking more befitting my
age and condition. Middle-aged actors shouldn't play
Hamlet. (*To prompter*) Although, *I* don't look middle-
aged, do I, Frank?

PROMPTER: Not anymore.

BARRYMORE: Insolent boy. Oh, cruelty, thy name is
Franklin. *Prompters!* So, it's Richard Crookback or
nothing. And if I don't do it, some other ham will
beat me to it. Right, Frank?

PROMPTER: Right, sir.

BARRYMORE: All right, let's get cracking.

(*He staggers*)

(*To audience*) You probably hadn't noticed, but I tend
to stagger. My whole family staggers. My father, God
rest his soul, was a great staggerer. "Staggering is a
sign of strength, Jackie," he'd say. "Only the weak
have to be carried home." (*To prompter*) Where were
we?

PROMPTER: Grim-visaged war—

BARRYMORE: Grim-visaged war hath smooth'd his wrinkled—(*Referring to apple*) Ethel sent me these. Red apples have been the Barrymore good luck wish—or the family curse—for generations.

I don't know why I ever went into theater. Lionel and I wanted to be painters—great painters of the American spirit, like Homer, Eakins, Whistler, Bellows. Ethel wanted to be a pianist. (*To prompter*) You may not know this, Frank, but I was for a time political cartoonist for the *Evening Journal*.

PROMPTER: Really, sir?

BARRYMORE: Oh, yes. Some of my happiest hours were spent at Minnie Hay's boarding house on 34th Street—a hangout for the tough newspaper crowd. Magnificent wastrels! (*As reporter*) Say, Jacko! How come ya always draw Teddy Roosevelt standin' in de tall grass? (*To reporter*) Because, my dear fellow, I never learned how to draw feet. (*To audience*) I also had one fatal flaw, which got me fired. All my drawings looked like me. The bad boy side I loved. So it was back to the stage. Dear old Ethel came to the rescue—got me a job.

But acting isn't an art. It's a scavenger profession, a junk pile of all the arts. It's just that we three were trapped in the family cul-de-sac. The Barrymores and the Drews! The Drews and the Barrymores! They wrote plays about us. We were the theater's Royal Family and I was the Clown Prince. Somewhere along the way, the public got tired of us. Can't

say I blame them. But it's paid well. That's the nar-
cotic. (*To prompter*) Frank?

PROMPTER: Yes, sir?

BARRYMORE: Do you think my fans will remember me
when I'm a has-been?

PROMPTER: Of course, they do, Mr. Barrymore.

BARRYMORE (*to audience*): I don't know what I'd do
without him, but I'd rather. (*To prompter*) Inciden-
tally, Frank, why haven't you been drafted?

PROMPTER: The Army didn't want me.

BARRYMORE: Why not?

PROMPTER: I'm 4-F.

BARRYMORE: Flat feet?

PROMPTER: No.

BARRYMORE: Weak eyes?

PROMPTER: No. Homosexual.

BARRYMORE: Yeah? Well, W.C. Fields and I were
turned down for Home Defense. You know what that
impudent girl behind the registration desk said?
"Who sent you, the enemy?"

W.C. replied, "Please correct me, if I'm wrong, my little hermaphrodite, but is that your truss that's chafing you, or is your tutu too tight?" (*Pause*) *Homosexual?* Did you have to tell them?

PROMPTER: I didn't.

BARRYMORE: Well, how did they know?

PROMPTER: I think they guessed.

BARRYMORE: Well, come to think of it—as W.C. would say—there *is* a bit of the tomboy in you, Frank. Damnit, you're a good man to own up to that. I must say, you've got guts. I'm proud of you. You're outspoken, honest, incredibly frank—Frank.

You know, the quaint irony of it is—I've sometimes wished I'd been born on your side of the fence. It's when I blamed women for my troubles and thought all dames were poison. Odd, that, considering I adore women more than do most men. Even though all four wives were bus accidents. Katherine, Dolores, Blanche—

PROMPTER: Didn't Blanche come *before* Dolores?

BARRYMORE: You're   right.   Katherine,   Blanche, Dolores—and *then* Eileen.

PROMPTER: Elaine.

BARRYMORE: Elaine. You're right. Funny how they all aspired to be actresses. Can you countenance that? But I think they loved me. I loved them. Yes, I did, God knows. But something tells me there won't be a fifth ex-Mrs. Barrymore. I would rather set fire to myself. (*Resuming Richard*) I,—that am not shap'd for sportive tricks—(*To prompter*) Frank?

PROMPTER: Yes?

BARRYMORE: I,—that am not shap'd for sportive tricks—

PROMPTER: Oh, uh—(*Finding the line*) Nor made to court an amorous—

BARRYMORE:
I,—that am not shap'd for sportive tricks,
Nor made to court an amorous looking-glass:
I, that am rudely stamp'd—line.

PROMPTER: And want love's majesty—

BARRYMORE: And want love's majesty—line.

PROMPTER: To strut—

BARRYMORE: To strut—

PROMPTER: Before a wanton—

BARRYMORE: Wanton—

PROMPTER: Ambling—

BARRYMORE: Ambling—

PROMPTER: Nymph—

BARRYMORE: What?

PROMPTER: Nymph!

BARRYMORE: Nymph! Katherine! My first. Blue mirrors for eyes, a taffy-haired debutante. Every vowel a dipthong—(*As Katherine*) Oh, you spilt lemonade all over my best white pique hat. (*To audience*) Foolish girl. For twenty years, Katherine and I were ecstatically happy. And then we met. (*To prompter*) Who came after her? Don't tell me. (*Pause*) Tell me.

PROMPTER: Blanche.

BARRYMORE: Blanche. That's right.

PROMPTER: Known as Michael.

BARRYMORE: Michael. That's right—

She was Blanche when I met her,
But wouldn't you know?
She changed into Michael,
A regular Joe.

19

She had the face of a Romney portrait and the soul of a marine. And she wrote free verse: "O noble Hercules, press me in your pungent arms."

And I did. She kindled fire in me. I kindled fire in her. We wore matching outfits. She looked like George Sand. *I* looked like George Sand.

It was then that Miss Sappho of 1920 hove into view like an oil tanker. Mercedes de Acosta. She doted on Blanche. Mercedes was more butch than Spartacus. God, who can forget her handshake? (*As Mercedes*) Ah, buenos dias, señor. Que hombre! And your wife, Miguel, que mujer! Ai-yi-yi! Put 'er there, señor. (*A crushing handshake*) Ai-yi-yi! (*To audience*) I don't have to tell you that divorces cost more than marriages, but, goddamnit! They're worth it! Lord, the shit I put myself through all those years. I don't mean just the marriages. Those absurd plays, all those flops! One goddamned cow pie after another.

And then Ned appears, my Warwick, my king-maker, my Voltaire. Ned Sheldon. Age twenty-five, a playwright, just out of Harvard, with a hit on Broadway. He sees me perform in some vapid little piece of fluff. (*As Ned*) Jack Barrymore, when are you going to stop wasting your talent? (*To Ned*) Talent? What talent? I'm in the family business, that's all. Like dry goods or hardware. (*As Ned*) No, no—but you don't realize what you're capable of. You could be doing the classics! (*To Ned*) The classics? Please! Tights? Prancing around the stage in some pantywaist getup? No, thank you. (*As Ned*) You're a coward,

Jack. Why are you so afraid? You know you've got everything—the looks, the heart, the ego *and* the talent. Oh, I admit, it's a little raw. You'll have to work your ass off. But if you do, you could be what the theater's searching for. You could be the next Edwin Booth. Come on, you flap-eared sonuvabitch! I'm going to get that Plantagenet nose of yours against some worthwhile grindstone. Are you game? (*To Ned*) Sure, I'm game. (*To audience*) Ned is as good as his word. He plots my career like a Roman general. He even writes plays for me. He got me started on Shakespeare. We were at the Bronx Zoo, mesmerized by a red tarantula with a gray bald spot on the back of its head, from trying to get out of the cage. Oh, God, what a sinister-looking thing. "Crawling power, Neddie," I said. "That reminds me of Richard the Third."

"Which you are going to play," he said. God bless you Ned. You made me reach for it. You even bought me a pet tarantula. (*To audience*) I called it Mercedes.

PROMPTER: Mr. Barrymore—

BARRYMORE (*to prompter*): Hold your horses, Frank. Hold your horses. (*To audience*) One summer, Ned and I rendezvoused in Venice. We wandered late at night across ancient bridges and deserted squares. We traveled the Grand Canal. We talked about everything under the sun. He talked, I listened. Then on to Florence. Our last night, in the cupola on top of our hotel roof, we waited for the sunrise.

As the dawn came, there it was in all its glory—the River Arno, the Uffizi Gallery, the Santa Croce Church of the Franciscans where Galileo and Michelangelo are buried. And there we were at four in the morning—singing to all of Florence—

(*Singing and dancing*)

When that midnight choo choo leaves for Alabam'
I'll be right there, I've got my fare.
When I see that rusty-haired conductor-man,
I'll grab him by the collar
And I'll holler
Alabam'! Alabam'!

(*To Ned*)

C'mon, Neddie, *dance*, you old bastard! I'm going to sit this one out. (*To audience*) I think he knew more about art and history than even old Ruskin himself. Ah, Ned—

Give me that man
That is not passion's slave, and I will wear him
In my heart's core, ay, in my heart of heart,
As I do thee.

That was one helluva summer.

Last summer they put me in a sanitarium. I forget where the hell it was. Somewhere out in the desert. Full of rich old boozers, who were there for the express purpose of drying out. A formidable creature named Frau Himmler was in charge. (*To Frau Himmler*) Ah, Frau Himmler, how enchanting you look. And how is Herr Himmler? (*As Frau Himmler*) Dead! Gone to Valhalla! (*To Frau Himmler*) In that case, my Teutonic tease, are you free to join me in a night cap? (*As Frau Himmler*) Zis ist a Clinic, Herr Berryman! Ve haf House Rules. Zere vill be no Schmoking, no Profanity und no Schmuggling in ze Schnapps by your Hollyvood riffraff Crowd! (*To Frau Himmler*) Then, perhaps, my Germanic Geranium, a little romp between the sheets? (*As Frau Himmler*) Schweinehund! Hanky-panky ist verboten! Zere vill be no Discussion of S.E.X. Vhat vas, vas. (*To Frau Himmler*) Have done thy charm, thou hateful wither'd hag! Up your Wienerschnitzel, you old Sauerkraut! (*To audience, admiring sword*) Ned gave me this. Sixteenth century. It's the real thing. I love old things—old friends, old times, old manners, old books, old trees, the old sun, the old moon, the old earth's face, old wine in dim flagons, old ships, old wagons. Where was I?

PROMPTER: In the sanitarium.

BARRYMORE: One night, when the Wagnerian Vixen was looking the other way, I escaped and joined a lady of the evening, a blushing flower who shall be nameless. Trixie Schumacher. Trixie's pushing forty from the wrong side, but she sparkles like a dental filling.

After a lively little game of jumble-giblets performed in the back seat of a taxi, we were quietly wassailing

23

in the cozy intimacy of a hotel dining room, when who should storm in but my old journalist friend, Gene Fowler. Gene immediately proceeded to berate, insult, and badmouth my poor, soiled little dove. I had no choice but to rise in defense of Trixie's honor.

"Now stop right there, Gene," I said. "I will not permit you to use such language in the presence of a whore!"

"Yer damn right!" said Trixie and hauled off and slapped him. She immediately regretted it. He was chewing tobacco. (*A paroxysm of laughing*) I gotta tell you this. Gene has a—Gene has a—Gene has a mother-in-law—

PROMPTER: Mr. Barrymore!

BARRYMORE: I gotta tell you this. Gene has a mother-in-law from hell! (*As Mumsie*) I can't understand grown men gettin' drunk and actin' like fools in front of decent people. Don't you bring that broken-down John Barrymore here anymore! (*To audience*) The fact is, he *did* bring me home early one morning before sunrise. (*As Gene*) Shh! Don't wake Mumsie. (*To audience*) As if I wanted to. While he was tiptoeing into the kitchen to get drinks, I got acquainted with Chester, Mumsie's beloved parrot. (*To parrot*) Say something, Chester. Don't just sit there, you stupid Technicolor chicken. (*To audience*) Turned out, the bird spoke nothing but French. (*As Chester, squawking*) Bon jour, madame, bwak! Bon jour, ma-

dame, bwak! Bon jour, madame, bwak! (*To audience*)
In no time, I had coached Chester in the King's En-
glish, downed my drink and departed. I was told that
later on when Mumsie passed his perch and sang
out, "Bon jour, Chester," the bird replied, "Bon jour,
madame, fuck you, bwak! Bon jour, madame, fuck
you, bwak!

Little drops of water,
Little blades of grass,
Once a noble actor,
Now a horse's ass.

(*He mimes Louella Parsons reading a news broadcast*)

Hello from Hollywood. This is Louella Parsons with
a scoop on that bad boy, John Barrymore. His latest
indiscretion took place last night at fashionable
Chasen's restaurant, where he relieved himself in a
potted palm next to a table of delegates from the
Daughters of the American Revolution. (*To audience*)
I don't remember the incident. I don't remember a
lot of things. Merciful amnesia. Fat-assed old gossip!
(*As Louella*) Jack Barrymore, will you kindly remember that I am a lady? (*To Louella*) Your secret is safe
with me, madam. (*To audience*) What a quaint old
udder she is. I never liked Louella, and I always will.

(*Back to Richard*)

I,—that am not shap'd for sportive tricks,
Nor made to court an amorous looking-glass;
I, that am rudely stamp'd—

BARRYMORE

PROMPTER: You've already done that, sir.

BARRYMORE: I know I have, but I like it! (*Resuming*) I, that am rudely stamp'd—line!

PROMPTER: And want love's majesty—

BARRYMORE:
And want love's majesty
To strut before a wanton ambling nymph;
I, that am—line?

PROMPTER: Curtail'd—

BARRYMORE:
I, that am curtail'd of this fair proportion,
Cheated of feature—line?

PROMPTER: By dissembling nature—

BARRYMORE: By dissembling nature—

PROMPTER: Deform'd—

BARRYMORE: Deform'd—

PROMPTER: Unfinish'd—

BARRYMORE: Don't tell me! (*Pause*) Tell me!

PROMPTER: Sent before my time—

26

BARRYMORE:
Sent before my time
Into this breathing world scarce half made up—
And that so lamely and unfashionable
That dogs bark at me as I halt by them.

Maybe I shouldn't wear these tights anymore. They originally belonged to Ethel. Lionel stole them and wore them for his Macbeth tights. When I got them, I wore them for my Richard tights, then my Hamlet tights. My dresser discreetly suggested that they be laundered—just once. (*To dresser*) Laundered, you irreverent lout? Have you no sense of tradition? I opened in these tights and, by God, I'll close in them! (*To audience*) When I die, I shall bequeath them to the Cathedral of San Giovanni Battista, to rest beside the Shroud of Turin.

A king am I of shreds and patches.

It's funny, the things I remember of my London opening of *Hamlet*. There I was, a callow youth of forty-three. I remember waiting in the wings, holding the theater cat in my arms. I called her my little Ophelia. Suddenly I hear my cue. It's too late. I have to carry her on with me. (*As Hamlet*) Get thee to a nunnery: or, if thou wilt needs marry, marry a fool; for wise men know well enough what monsters you make of them. To a nunnery, go; and quickly too. Farewell. (*To audience*) Then afterwards, everyone gone—(*To prompter*) Frank, dim the lights.

PROMPTER: What for?

BARRYMORE: I want to feel that chill again. (*To audience*) I waited till the theater was dark and empty. Then I walked out onto the Haymarket stage and stood there all alone—except for the ghosts.

(*Lights dim*)

(*As Hamlet*)
To be, or not to be—that is the question:
Whether 'tis nobler in the mind to suffer
The slings and arrows of outrageous fortune,
Or to take arms against a sea of troubles
And by opposing end them? To die, to sleep—
No more—and by a sleep to say we end
The heart-ache and the thousand natural shocks
That flesh is heir to. 'Tis a consummation
Devoutly to be wish'd. To die, to sleep;
To sleep, perchance to dream.
(*To audience*)
You know, there's one moment in a lifetime when all the stars seem to gather together and become one— and that moment belongs to you. It was there on that dark stage that I suddenly saw it could all be mine— if I wanted it. But the moment wouldn't wait for me. It passed me by.

(*Lights bounce up again*)

Jesus, Frank! You scared the shit out of me. What the hell's going on? Why'd you do that?

PROMPTER: We're wasting time.

BARRYMORE: Says who?

PROMPTER: Says *me*—sir. We've only got the place for one night.

BARRYMORE: Stop bullying me! I want to tell them my story.

PROMPTER: What story?

BARRYMORE: The dowager story.

PROMPTER: Oh, God, *that* one. Well, make it fast.

BARRYMORE: All right, Frank. Thank you very much. I'm so sorry. I'll be with you in a minute. (*To audience*) During the run, a dowager accosted me. (*As dowager*) Mr. Barrymore, I do beg your pardon, but in your opinion, did Hamlet have sexual relations with Ophelia? (*To dowager*) In my opinion, madam, no. Though I hear—in a certain Chicago company— Hamlet had fellatio with Horatio. (*To audience*) On the opening night, however, George Bernard Shaw came to see this American upstart fall flat on his face. He very kindly delivered his opinion of me by letter, instead of to the press. I call it "The Shavian Upper-cut." I carry it here, next to my heart—(*Reading note*) Hi, Handsome—I'm free after the show for fun and—

Oh, no, that's not it.

(*Finds Shaw's letter*)

29

My dear Mr. Barrymore, I thank you for inviting me to your first London performance of *Hamlet*. You saved an hour and a half by the cutting, and filled it up with an interpolated drama of your own dumb show. I wish you would concentrate on acting, rather than authorship, at which, believe me, the Bard can write your head off. Yours perhaps too candidly, G.B.S. (*To audience*) No, damn it! I was a hit! "Haymaker at the Haymarket." That's what the London critics wrote.

Listen, you fat-headed Fabian, in those halcyon days I had ideals! I reveled in being compared to men like Keane, Mansfield, Booth. One of my greatest regrets will always be that I couldn't sit in an audience and watch me perform. That doesn't sound conceited, does it? (*To prompter*) Does it, Frank?

PROMPTER: No.

BARRYMORE: Of course, it doesn't. (*To audience*) I held on to those ideals. You have to, when you're up there. If I wasn't going to be a painter, at least I could try to master the family business—Papa's business. Ah, Papa!

Maurice Barrymore. Christened Herbert Arthur Chamberlayne Hunter Blyth, complete with Oxford accent, monocle, and silk topper. In spite of what I thought of him, I tried so hard to emulate his voice. But I had an unfortunate furry rasp in mine. "Jackie's a disgrace to the family," he would say.

"Sounds like he's been sleeping with those barkers on Coney Island."

Little did he know that at fourteen, I was sleeping with his second wife—my stepmother Mamie. Her diction was impeccable. She assured me it was my duty to take Papa's place in bed while he was away. She said it would be good for my diction. (*To Mamie*) Are you sure, Mamie? (*As Mamie*) Yes, Jackie, you'll see. We'll practice very hard. Now, crawl under the blanket with me and lie back. Relax. (*To Mamie*) Excuse me, but what's this got to do with diction, Mamie? (*As Mamie*) Lie back, do as I say. Don't be so tense. Here, let me guide your hand. Say after me—

Francis Finch's frugal father, Floyd,
Was fond of fondling feckless Phyllis Pfeiffer,
Flaming floozy from filthy foggy Fairfield.

Faster, Jackie! Faster!

Francis Finch's frugal father, Floyd,
Was fond of fondling feckless Phyllis Pfeiffer,
Flaming floozy from filthy foggy Fairfield.

Now, try it again, Jackie. Keep the rhythm going. Let's do it together.

(*Rapidly*)

Francis Finch's frugal father, Floyd,
Was fond of f-f-f-f-f-f-f-f-f-f-f-

(*To audience*)

Suddenly, the door flew open! Papa came in! (*As Papa*) Jackie! (*To Papa*) Fapa! Mamie was just felping me with my fiction! (*As Papa*) Splendid, my boy! You sound better already. (*To audience*) That was Papa.

I hardly remember my mother. She died when I was so young. A fine comedienne, Papa would say. But *her* mother. That's another story.

Grandma Drew. She called me her little Greengoose—"like the pretty lad in the storybook." We called her Mum Mum. She sent me to kindergarten at the convent school. One day I threw an egg at another little boy. Mum Mum rebuked me.

(*As Mum Mum*) Now, look here, Greengoose, one day you may become an actor like your daddy, and the egg will be thrown back at you. (*To audience*) I think Mum Mum was a great actress. She was also the first woman to head a major American theater, the Arch Street Theatre in Philadelphia. Eventually, she lost it. She lost everything. She didn't seem to mind.

Before she died, she said, "You children are my pride and joy. Ethel will be the luminous one. She has starlight on her head. Lionel will be the stable, solid, practical one. But you, Greengoose, you will dream too long and too deep, and one day be gravely hurt by your awakening."

We lived in her Twelfth Street house which we called "The Tomb of the Capulets"—a Victorian monstrosity with cavernous halls, monastic rooms and two attics, where Lionel and I slept. Up the long, dimly-lit staircase to bed I'd go, scared to death of the gloom ahead. (*To Mum Mum*) I don't want to go up there, Mum Mum. It's too dark. (*To audience*) She'd call to me from the foot of the stairs—(*As Mum Mum*) You needn't worry, Greengoose. There's nothing to be afraid of. Nothing can hurt you. You have a wonderful power. Say that after me. You can't hurt me. I have a wonderful power. Say it again and again. Keep on saying it. (*To Mum Mum*) You can't hurt me. I have a wonderful power. You can't hurt me. I have a wonderful power. G'night, Mum Mum.

I'm coming up, Lionel, be careful. Don't break another window. They'll blame me. God, it's black up there. Come on, let's go find the secret passage.

Where the hell am I? (*Seeing prompter*) Who's that over there, standing in the wings? (*To audience*) Would someone tell me who the hell that is? (*To prompter*) What're you staring at?

PROMPTER: It's just me. Frank.

BARRYMORE: Oh, yeah. Frank. (*To audience*) Guess I took a little detour there. Goddamn, he looked so familiar. For a minute, I couldn't think who he was. (*To prompter*) Frank?

PROMPTER: Yes.

BARRYMORE

BARRYMORE: Were you on a break?

PROMPTER: No, sir.

BARRYMORE: Who said you could take a break?

PROMPTER: But I didn't—

BARRYMORE: Where *were* you? (*To audience*) Where
are they when you need them? (*As Richard*) If you
do fight against your country's—line!

PROMPTER: Uh—your country's foes—

BARRYMORE: If you do fight in safeguard of your—line!

PROMPTER: Your wives—

BARRYMORE: Your wives shall—what? What's the line,
Frank? Your wives shall—what?

PROMPTER: Your wives shall welcome—but that's not
Richard's line, sir!

BARRYMORE: Well, whose is it?

PROMPTER: Richmond's.

BARRYMORE: I'll take it!

PROMPTER: Your wives shall welcome home the con-
querors.

BARRYMORE: My wives wouldn't welcome me home, if
I came bearing the Holy friggin' Grail! Each marriage lasted seven years, like a skin rash. My troubles
don't come from chasing women. They come from
catching them. The trouble is—everyone wants to
put halos over my unworthy head and then hold
them up with broomsticks. Pretty soon they get tired
of holding up the broomsticks. For Ned Sheldon I
don't need a goddamned halo. He doesn't need a
broomstick. (*To Ned*) What the hell are you, Neddie?
What prank of irony made you my friend? What
made you stoop to serve this wretch, this buffoon,
this counterfeit of a man? (*To audience*) He's always
trying to save me, but I never listen. And now, like
Richard, I'm lost—

(*As Richard*)
   Seeking a way, and straying from the way;
   Not knowing how to find the open air,
   But toiling desperately to find it out,—
   And from that torment I will free myself,
   Or hew my way out with a bloody axe.
   Why, I can smile, and murder whiles I smile;
   And cry content to that which grieves my heart;
   And wet my cheeks with artificial tears,
   And frame my face to all occasions.
   I'll drown more sailors than the mermaid shall;
   I'll play the orator as well as Nestor;
   Deceive more slily than Ulysses could;
   And, like a Sinon, take another Troy:
   I can add colours to the cameleon;
   Change shapes with Proteus for advantages;
   And set the murderous Machiavel to school.

BARRYMORE

Can I do this, and cannot get a crown?
Tut, were it further off, I'll pluck it down!

(*To prompter*) Where's the nearest toilet, Frank?

PROMPTER: Just off stage right, sir.

BARRYMORE: Thank you.

PROMPTER: Down one flight—

BARRYMORE: Yes.

PROMPTER: Turn left at the fire extinguisher.

BARRYMORE: Nowhere closer? An open window, perchance? A sink? A cuspidor? A jardiniere? A potted palm? Preferably near a D.A.R. delegation. (*To audience*) You will excuse me for a brief interval? This is, after all, an emergency. (*Heading offstage; as Richard*) Shine out, fair sun, till I have bought a glass, that I may see my shadow as I piss!

PROMPTER: Pass!

BARRYMORE: Pass! (*He exits.*)

Act Two

ACT II

Same set. Two hours later. The throne is now in evidence, a crown resting beside it. Barrymore as Richard enters. He is costumed and wigged. As if in hellish torment and with measured steps, he slowly makes his lurching way to the throne, where he wearily sits.

BARRYMORE: Wynken, Blynken and Nod one night— (*To prompter*) Frank, I'm paying you to prompt me!

PROMPTER: You're paying me?

BARRYMORE: Don't get cute, Frank.

PROMPTER: I don't care about the money.

BARRYMORE: What?

PROMPTER: I just want you to do *Richard.*

BARRYMORE: How can I do it, unless you prompt me?

PROMPTER: I *have* been prompting you.

BARRYMORE: Then, I can't hear you.

PROMPTER: What?

BARRYMORE: You're on the wrong side.

PROMPTER: Wrong side?

BARRYMORE: I don't like you there. I like you over there. You should be on stage right. No wonder I'm forgetting lines. It's all your fault. Oh, stupid boy! Hie thee to stage right forthwith, or by my troth, I'll knock your leek about your pate.

PROMPTER: Gotcha.

(*We hear the prompter's footsteps running across the back of the stage to stage right*)

BARRYMORE: Gotcha. Impudent jackanapes. The Great Profile is not this side—but *this*. Say, who started the notion—big nose, big dick?

Queen Johanna of Naples! Jumbo Johanna. A lady of unbridled lust—sized up a man's nose, and if she liked what she saw, brazenly groped him, while murmuring in his ear, "Nasatorum peculio." Latin for "big nose, big hose." (*To prompter*) Have you landed yet, Frank?

PROMPTER (*now at stage right*): Ready when you are, sir.

BARRYMORE: Ready.

PROMPTER: Richard's in his tent.

BARRYMORE: Right.

PROMPTER: It's the night before the battle.

BARRYMORE: What battle?

PROMPTER: Bosworth Field.

BARRYMORE: Right. Is this all the light we're gonna get?

PROMPTER: Yes.

BARRYMORE: Well, all right. Sound ready to go?

PROMPTER: Yes, sir.

BARRYMORE: Then, give me some wind, Frank. (*Wind sound, very loud*) Not a typhoon! Bring it down. (*Wind down*) That's better.

PROMPTER: You're supposed to be asleep, sir.

BARRYMORE: Oh. (*Snoring*) Get me started.

PROMPTER: But you didn't say "line."

BARRYMORE: I'm asleep. What comes next?

PROMPTER: The ghosts appear—

BARRYMORE: Yes.

PROMPTER: The ghosts vanish—

BARRYMORE: Yeah.

PROMPTER: Richard wakes.

BARRYMORE (*acting*):   Give me another horse! Bind up my wounds! Let's get outta here! No, that's not right. Cut! (*To prompter*) Let's start again. Quiet on the set! Is this my close-up? What lens is that—a 75? Don't forget the filter. Quiet! Roll 'em. (*Acting*) Give me another horse! Give me another horse! (*To audience*) How many horses does this guy need? Will someone throw me a line? A line! A line! My kingdom for a line! I can't see the goddamned blackboards from here. My career's gonna be on the floor with John Gilbert's, if I don't get this right.

John Gilbert, that poor guy. There he was, top of the heap, Hollywood's number one he-man, romantic rogue, lover, swashbuckler, one of the great stars of the silent screen. Then he made his first talking picture, and everyone found that—(*Gilbert's high voice*)—he talked like this. (*To audience*) He came to me, bewildered—cried on my shoulder—(*As Gilbert*) What's happened to my career? They turned on me, Jack. Why? Why? (*To Gilbert*) Listen to yourself, you white-livered runagate! Are you deaf? (*To audience*) Poor Johnny. Finita la commedia. (*Back to his scene*) Right! Roll 'em! (*Acting*) I turn my body from the sun. Towards thee I roll, thou all-destroying but unconquering whale. (*To himself*) That's not right. Who was that? Ahab? Jekyll? Hyde? (*As Svengali*) I remember nothing, I see nothing, I hear nothing, I dream of nothing but Svengali, Svengali, Svengali, Svengali! (*To audience*) *My* ghosts.

PROMPTER: Are you lost, Mr. Barrymore?

BARRYMORE (*to prompter*): Am I lost? Do they sell flowers on Mother's Day? Yes, I'm lost.

PROMPTER: Wherefore—

BARRYMORE: Because I can't remember, damnit!

PROMPTER: "Wherefore" is the cue, sir.

BARRYMORE: Oh. (*To audience*) "Wherefore" is the cue. (*To prompter*) Well, give it a little louder, sweetheart. I can't hear you. (*Putting on crown*) So far I've only needed a hundred and six prompts. Where the hell did you get this goddamned thing?

PROMPTER: RKO.

BARRYMORE: RKO? Well, it's too small. Or my head's too big. My temples are throbbing like hell. Perchance it is tomorrow morning's hangover making a premature appearance. God, Frank, I had the most frightening thought while sitting on the can.

PROMPTER: What was that?

BARRYMORE: If I don't pay alimony next month, can my wives repossess me? Well, can they?

PROMPTER: I doubt it, sir.

BARRYMORE: I sincerely hope you're right, Frank, because I consider it the most exorbitant of stud fees. And the worst feature of it is—you pay retroactively.

I spend my entire time trying to scare off the hyenas
snapping at my heels with writs and summonses,
waiting to tear every last bit of flesh from my bat-
tered bones. Quite frankly, Frank, I've been pauper-
ized. Fortunately, I have enough money to last me
the rest of my life, provided I drop dead right now.

(*He starts the victrola record*)

(*Singing*)
You must have been a beautiful baby,
You must have been a wonderful child.
When you were only startin' to go to kindergarten,
I bet you drove the little boys wild—
(*To audience*)
Gad, I could've written this!
(*Singing*)
And when it came to winning blue ribbons,
You must have shown the other kids how,
I can see the judges' eyes as they handed you the
prize,
I bet you made the cutest bow.
Oh! You must have been a beautiful baby,
'Cause baby look at you now.

Have you noticed that Wagner had the decency to
write his Wedding March in the tempo of a dirge?

But the truth is, I could fall in love again, just like
that. The one thing in the world that still excites me
is a woman. How divine a thing. How I miss them.
Most of all, wife number three. Beautiful Dolores.

My one truly happy marriage. She made such a success of it, I had to get out.

So, we'll go no more a-roving
So late into the night,
Though the heart be still as loving,
And the moon be still as bright.

For the sword outwears its sheath,
And the soul wears out the breast,
And the heart must pause to breathe,
And Love itself have rest.

When wife number four divorced me, she said, "Jack, I'm sorry, but you don't have the qualities I want in a man."

I said, "Elaine, my drear, if I had the qualities you want in a man, I'd have married someone else." Funny—our honeymoon seems like yesterday, and you know what a lousy day yesterday was. But, between you, me and the lamppost, I wasn't good enough for any of my wives. But I didn't tell them. I let it come as a surprise. (*To prompter*) Frank, you wouldn't by any chance have something to drink, would you?

PROMPTER: 'Scuse me, sir?

BARRYMORE: A little tonsillar lubrication?

PROMPTER: What?

BARRYMORE

BARRYMORE: Something to wet my whistle.

PROMPTER: Oh—yes, sir.

BARRYMORE: Good.

PROMPTER: I have just the thing.

BARRYMORE (*to audience*):   A little drinkee-poo.

PROMPTER: A nice glass of milk.

BARRYMORE: Oh. I once drank a glass of milk—ten years ago—and when it reached my stomach, it turned into a suede glove.

PROMPTER: Maybe we should get on with it, sir.

BARRYMORE: Yes, maybe we should, Frank, maybe we should. You're right. Where were we? Where were we? Oh, God, I shall despair.

PROMPTER: That's right.

BARRYMORE: What?

PROMPTER: "I shall despair"—that's the line.

BARRYMORE: That's the line? "I shall despair?"

PROMPTER: Yes. So say it.

BARRYMORE: What?

46

PROMPTER: Stop stalling and say the line! I know you can do this. You're wasting time.

BARRYMORE: Now, wait a minute!

PROMPTER: Wait a minute? That's all I've been doing—*waiting!*

BARRYMORE: All you've been doing is whining!

PROMPTER: Just say the line! Cut the bullshit!

BARRYMORE: Who the hell do you think you're talking to?

PROMPTER: You—you miserable old ham!

BARRYMORE: Well, screw you, you nasty little faggot! I was a good Richard!

PROMPTER: No! You weren't!

BARRYMORE: What?

(*Beat*)

PROMPTER: You were a *great* Richard.

BARRYMORE: Yeah?

PROMPTER: You were a great Hamlet.

BARRYMORE: Yeah? Well, what happened to me? (*As Hamlet*) I have of late,—but wherefore I know not,—lost all my mirth, forgone all custom of exercises; and, indeed, it goes so heavily with my disposition that this goodly frame, the earth, seems to me a sterile promontory; this most excellent canopy, the air, look you, this brave o'erhanging firmament, this majestical roof fretted with golden fire,—why it appears no other thing to me than a foul and pestilent congregation of vapours. What a piece of work is man! How noble in reason! How infinite in faculties! In form and moving, how express and admirable! In action, how like an angel! In apprehension, how like a god! The beauty of the world! The paragon of animals! And yet, to me, what is this quintessence of dust? Man delights not me; no, nor woman neither, though by your smiling you seem to say so.

PROMPTER: I wasn't smiling, sir.

BARRYMORE: I know that, Frank.

PROMPTER: Shall we get back to Richard?

BARRYMORE: I'd like to get back to something. I want to be something, whatever the goddamned role. I have to convince myself that the lines I speak are mine, because I speak them. How else am I going to peer into the wings filled with stagehands in dirty undershirts, crates, dust, clutter and junk—and say fervently, "Come to the window, Cynthia. Observe the crescent moon rising over the sea."

And then, there's the audience. Ay, there's the rub. Whether it's Barnum & Bailey or Broadway, they're still the same great hulking monster with two thousand eyes and twenty thousand teeth, breathing out there in the darkness, withholding, teasing, waiting—waiting to make or break men like me. Oh, that darkness! That darkness. (*Glancing in mirror*) Christ! This is obviously going to be a vintage Richard. Perhaps I should've snuck up to the mirror. For a moment, I thought it was my father.

You know, when I do a picture, I try to get Bill Daniels. He's the best cameraman I know. He makes these oxen dewlaps disappear. Garbo won't make a picture without him. When we shot Grand Hotel at MGM, Bill got rid of these sweetbreads under my eyelids and this moose's lavaliere.

Ah, vanity! Of course, Lionel isn't vain. Lucky fellow. He doesn't give a damn how he looks onscreen. I've made five pictures with my brother. He's always nagging at the director—(*As Lionel*) Now look here! I know Jack is doing all sorts of treacherous things behind my back to steal scenes, rolling his eyeballs or showing his goddamned profile. (*To audience*) That's a laugh. Lionel is the master upstager. Our last picture together was *Night Flight*. The big scene was all mine. There wasn't a chance in hell that Lionel could steal it. The director bet me ten smackers that he couldn't manage it this time. The cameras started grinding away. I had all the dialogue. Lionel turned his back to the camera, walked to the door for his exit, and just as he got there—he reached around and scratched his ass. There's a brother to be proud of.

Poor Lionel. He's broken his hip twice and is now confined to a wheelchair. Poor Lionel? What am I saying? It's the best gimmick an actor ever had, and he agrees with me. (*As Lionel*) Jack, nothing greater could have been contrived for me than the character of the grouchy but likable old grandfather in a wheelchair. As a result, I'm now a first class hypochondriac, and I'm enjoying it immensely. (*To audience*) He's always been a hypochondriac. He feels bad when he feels good, because he knows he'll feel worse when he feels better. God bless my brother. Back in '23 he told me he was getting engaged to be married a second time. "Not Irene," I said. "Jesus, how awkward!" (*As Lionel*) What's awkward about that, you miserable jackass? (*To Lionel*) I happen to have been to bed with her myself. (*To audience*) He didn't speak to me for ten years. Oh, well, we made up at last. He's always nagging at me—(*As Lionel*) Jack, you're such a snob about pictures. They're so much easier than the theater. When a movie's finished, your performance is in the can. (*To audience*) Or in the toilet. Of course, Ethel doesn't approve, but then, that's Ethel. (*As Ethel*) Oh, Jack, Jack, you've sold out to Hollywood. Come back, come back to your home in the theater. Come back! Come back! (*To Ethel*) Oh, Ethel, go fuck a duck. You, too, Lionel. (*To audience*) It's all so ridiculous. Broadway versus Hollywood, Hollywood versus Broadway. What's there to compare? Sodom with subways or

Gomorrah with palm trees—it's all the same. (*Disdainfully*) *Movies!*

PROMPTER: What were you last in, Mr. Barrymore?

BARRYMORE: I believe it was Joan Crawford.

(*Beat*)

Oh! What *movie!* I can't recall, thank God. Something for RKO. Of course, my trustworthy blackboards were strewn all over the set. "Goddamn it, Jackie," yelled the director, "why don't you learn your lines like everyone else?" (*To director*) Because, Anatol, precious, my memory is full of beauty—Paradise Lost, the Queen Mab speech, the great Sonnets. Do you expect me to clutter up my mind with donkey doo-doo? (*To audience*) Those kidney-faced baboons for whom I labor are some of the most ignorant, uncultured asses in the world. "Are you sure you want to make that picture?" I said to Sam Goldwyn. "You know, it's about two lesbians." (*As Goldwyn*) So? We'll make 'em Americans.

PROMPTER: Come on, Mr. Barrymore.

BARRYMORE: What do you want, Frank? What do you want?

PROMPTER: We're wasting time.

BARRYMORE: What the hell do you care? You're getting paid for it.

BARRYMORE

PROMPTER (*angrily*):   Okay, that's it!

BARRYMORE: That's what?

PROMPTER: I've had it!

BARRYMORE: Where the hell do you think you're go-ing?

PROMPTER: I'm getting my coat. I quit!

BARRYMORE: Frank—

PROMPTER: You are a spoiled child! You've always gotten everything you wanted. Now you can't have it. You're not going to do Richard. You haven't got the guts. You're worse than a drunk—you're a coward!

(*We hear the prompter's footsteps crossing*)

BARRYMORE (*dazed*):   Jesus. There's the whistle. They know I'm crazy. (*Imploringly*) Don't go, Frank! Don't go. Help me, please. Help me. I've got to finish this, or they'll put me away. Come back, come back. I'll try again. I promise—I'll try, I'll try. You just watch me. I have a wonderful power!

All you host of heaven! O earth! What else?
And shall I couple hell? Hold, my heart;
And you, my sinews. Grow not instant old,
But bear me stiffly up.—Remember thee!

Ay, thou poor ghost, while memory holds a seat
In this distracted globe—

while memory holds—

No, no, no, no, no. It's not working. It's not working.
It's no good, no good. I can't do it, Mum Mum. I
can't do it anymore. What's the line? What's the
line? What's the line? (*Long pause*) Frank? Frank?
Frank? Still there? Frank?

PROMPTER (*from stage left*):   Still here.

BARRYMORE: Did you know my father wrote his own
epitaph?

PROMPTER: No.

BARRYMORE: Well, he did.

He walked beneath the stars
And slept beneath the sun;
He lived a life of going-to-do
And died with nothing done.

(*To audience*)

I had to commit him to Bellevue. He was only fifty-
one. A lethal combination of absinthe and syphilis. At
his burial, the straps around his coffin got twisted, so
they had to hoist the whole goddamned thing up
again. How like Papa—a curtain call. (*To prompter*)

Frank, I really think I'm going to need something to drink. I'm getting the shakes again.

PROMPTER: Would you like some black coffee?

BARRYMORE: No.

PROMPTER: May I ask you something?

BARRYMORE: Go right ahead, Frank.

PROMPTER: Well, why don't you try AA?

BARRYMORE: Hell, why not? I'll drink anything. (*To audience*) You're not fooling me. You're boozers, all of you. I can tell. Your faces are blurred.

(*He breaks down briefly*)

PROMPTER: Sir? Are you all right?

BARRYMORE: No, I am not all right, thank you. I'm waylaid by regrets. I can't go back to that room in the sky, to childhood, to anything. I've pissed it all away. There's nowhere to go. I can't stop running.

I fled Him, down the nights and down the days;
I fled Him, down the arches of the years;
I fled Him, down the labyrinthine ways
Of my own mind; and in the mist of tears
I hid from Him, and under running laughter,
From those strong Feet that followed, followed
after.

Well, Richard, Hamlet—all my pals, I'm free of you
now. (*Pause*) She called to me from the foot of the
stairs. (*As Mum Mum*) I saw you come into this
world, Greengoose, and now you're seeing me out.
That's a fair exchange. (*To Mum Mum*) Oh, Mum
Mum, don't say that. (*As Mum Mum*) Oh, but it's
true. Actors are like waves of the sea. They rise to
separate heights, then break on the shore and are
gone, unremembered. Nothing as dead as a dead actor. Nothing. Not even a doornail. (*To prompter*) You
can douse the lights now.

PROMPTER: What'd you say?

BARRYMORE: You heard me.

PROMPTER: You can't quit now.

BARRYMORE: Do as I say!

PROMPTER: No! I won't let you.

BARRYMORE: Unarm!

PROMPTER: No!

BARRYMORE:
  Unarm! The long day's task is done,
  And we must sleep.
  No more a soldier.—Bruised pieces, go;
  My treasure's in the harbour, take it.
  Leave me, I pray, a little: pray you now:—
  Nay, do so; for, indeed, I have lost command.

BARRYMORE

(*To audience*)

And if you want to avoid domestic strife, don't marry in January. And that goes for the other months, too.

PROMPTER: But, sir—you haven't come to the end.

BARRYMORE (*to prompter*):   Oh, yes, I have. I won't fool myself any longer. Vat vas, vas. And *you* don't fool me, either.

PROMPTER: What?

BARRYMORE: I know who you are. *He* sent you, didn't he? The man in the bright nightgown. You've come for me, haven't you? But I'm damned if I'll go quietly. I have a wonderful power!

(*To audience*)

I was ever a fighter, so—one fight more,
The best and the last!
I would hate that death bandaged my eyes, and forbore,
And bade me creep past.

PROMPTER: Mr. Barrymore, don't you want your apples?

BARRYMORE: No, no, you keep them. No more red apples for me. (*To audience*) Jesus, if only Eve had offered Adam a daiquiri, we'd still be in Paradise. (*He exits.*)

The End